NURSERY SCHOOL SCIENCE

F. Pervaiz

Published by
Sunrise Publications
43 Glastonbury Court, Talbot Road, London W13, UK
© Copyright: Sunrise Publications
First printed in 1990
Reprinted March 1994

Illustrations by Glenn Goodwin

Printed by Jolly & Barber Printing Limited

ISBN 0 9515248 0 1

To all teachers

All experiments have been done with children, I have not written anything without trying it in the classroom first.

All experiments are done in a very systematic way, nothing haphazard. I believe that a correct approach to learning science should be established right from the start.

Children have enjoyed all experiments, this is extremely important.

There has not been any direct teaching or giving of "hard facts".

The sort of learning environment I provided enabled children to ask questions. Some I answered and some I ignored beautifully i.e. I could not give the right explanation when a child asked me why some things float while others sink because the correct answer would have been to difficult for him to understand and I never give "distorted facts" or wrong explanations, that is not laying down a good foundation for learning of science.

Work on plant and animal life is particularly aimed at children living in inner cities, flats, etc., who miss out on this very important aspect of learning.

One needs to imagine all sorts of things that children may be able to "get up to" while planning a science activity and take necessary precautions. Hands must be washed after touching animals, planting seeds etc.

The experiments with iron filings on pages 23, 24, 25, 26 require a teacher to be sitting with the children, there should not be more than two children at a time.

A lot of work I have done fits in with the usual nursery activities of number, colour, comparing, sorting, matching and categorizing.

CONTENTS

PLANTS

Making the name go funny

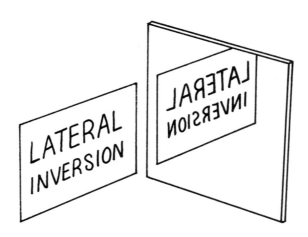

This experiment is suitable for children who can read their names. The whole point of this activity is to show that things change in the mirror, we do not go over how and why. Children read their name and then tried reading it in the mirror, to their surprise the name had gone "funny" as they put it, except one girl who did *"mirror writing"* said it looks better now.

Making a car go faster

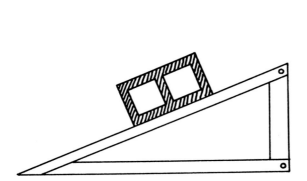 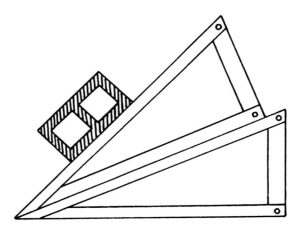

a) Children did not understand the principal, but they did the right thing by trial and error. The aim was to make the car (a wheel-less one which they made from Mobilo construction toys) go down the triangular block faster. They achieved this by placing another block underneath it. Though they could not explain that it was due to the increased angle of inclination, next time they come across something similar, they would know how to cope with the problem.

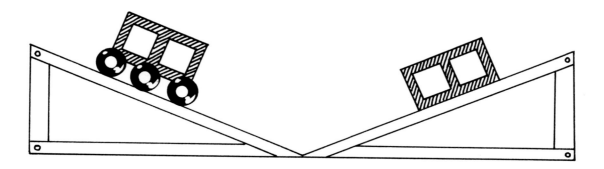

b) We had two triangular blocks and children were not allowed to raise any of the two by placing another block, as in the previous experiment. The question was how to make the car (wheel-less) go faster. I showed them a normal car which went faster, children were quick to point out the difference — *WHEELS,* and so wheels were added to the (Mobilo) cars and the experiment worked quite well. With both experiments (a) and (b) I provided the children with the right play material, discussed and helped them to think and do the right thing.

Mirror and images

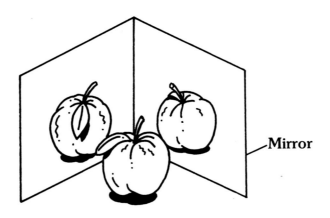

Mirror

Two mirrors were hinged together with cellotape, an object was placed in front of the mirror (four children did this experiment at a time – 4 pairs of mirrors). When the mirrors were straight at an angle of 180°, there was only one image of the object, but as the angle was decreased the number of images increased. Children tried placing different sorts of objects i.e. a bead, a little block, they even used their hands and also kept changing the angle between the mirrors and counting the images. Children described the effect as magic. We did not use glass mirrors, it was some silvered plastic material. Apart from the science experience it is a number exercise.

Headless dolly

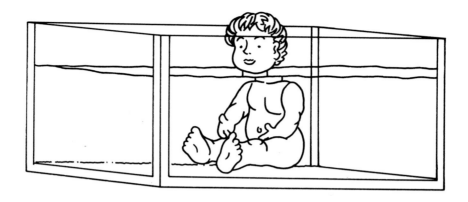

We filled an empty fish tank with water and placed a doll in it. The doll was fairly light and started floating, so we had to put metal chains around her to keep her down. The water was up to the neck of the doll. Children looked at the doll and some said her head is broken (it did appear to have moved to one side). I took the dolly out of the water, and the head was properly stuck on the neck. One of the children said that it is the water that makes the dolly's head look broken, they all agreed, and that was what I was trying to get across.

Making a rainbow

This is as simple as placing a transparent container of water near the window, rays of sunlight when they fall on the water produce a rainbow below. If a mirror is placed in the container then the rainbow is made on the ceiling. We used a glass fish tank and a tray with a mirror placed in a slanting position fixed with plasticine. These were placed in front of a window, (rays of sun must fall directly on the water). Fish tank produced a straight long rainbow, A.

Making a rainbow

Tray with mirror produced rainbow on the ceiling, B. Then I showed the children a prism that produced the same colours. Most will in their minds, connect rainbow with water and sun's rays, because this was left for about a week, and when it was cloudy there were no rainbows, children would occasionally ask me what happened to the rainbows, and I would say "Get the sun out if you want rainbows."

Matching game with shadows

We used overhead projector for producing shadows. It is very simple, it just means placing shapes, flat ones, such as plastic triangles, squares, animal templates which are always found in nurseries, or any other shapes made out of cardboard or thin wood, on the glass, which throws a nice shadow of that object on the wall or screen. The size of the shadow can be changed by moving the projector backward or forward. From the shadow children had to tell me the name of the object. This was an enjoyable matching game, and it also made them aware of the fact that objects can have shadows.

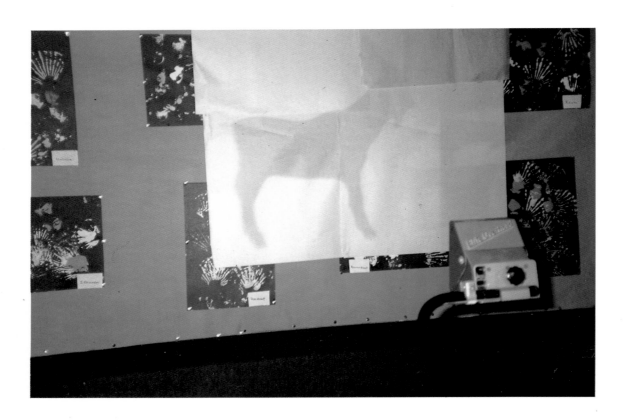

Making pictures with food colourings

We used wet paper towels, pipettes and different coloured food dyes in small bottles. Some we took just as they came, some we made by mixing the two or three together ourselves. We placed the wet paper towels on plastic glass, children then put a few drops of food colouring on it (one has to be very careful here, they tend to use too much). Drops of food colouring spread on the paper towel producing a nice rainbow effect. One doesn't need to explain anything, (chromotography is too difficult) but it should be done just for the sake of a pleasant colourful experience, besides they learn the name of colours so easily this way.

Blue and pink

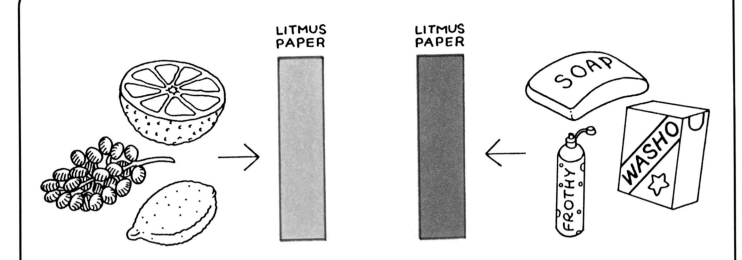

This in my opinion is the nicest way of teaching blue and pink colours, they learn the name "litmus paper", and the fact that it can change colour, pink to blue and vice versa. This activity was enjoyed by lots of children. An adult is needed to supervise the activity, they cannot get on with it by themselves. Litmus paper can be ordered through a science catalogue. It is an organic dye on paper, and turns blue in alkaline substances and pink in acid. I took lots of things from everyday use:- fruit, i.e. lemon, apple, orange, grapefruit, grapes, yoghurt, onion, tomato, they are all acidic, and alkaline substances like washing powder, toilet soap, dishwashing powder etc. etc. By the end of the session they all knew pink and blue colour.

Making pictures with sweets

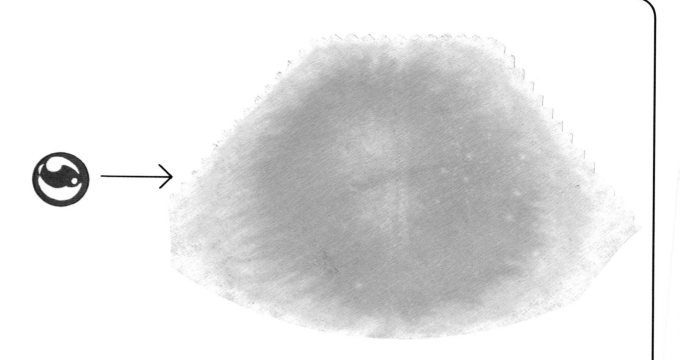

Children took a drop of water in a spoon and placed a Smartie in it and then transferred it on to the filter paper, (filter paper is the type used in preparing coffee), they chose their own Smartie and made a guess at the colour they were going to get on the filter paper, and then saw what they got. It was great fun, this also helped in learning of colours. We used Smarties but any multicoloured sweet should do, one needs to experiment a little with sweets before doing this activity with children.

Hot and cold–Introducing thermometer

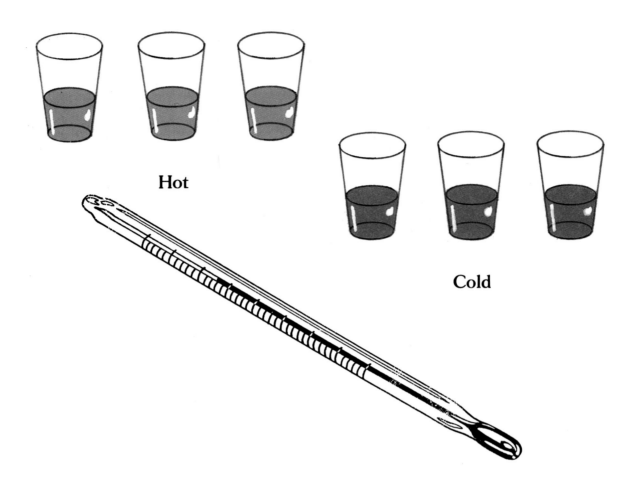

Hot

Cold

This was done at various levels depending on age/ability of the child. We had three glasses of blue coloured water varying in temperature from iced water, cold fridge water to ordinary tap water, and three glasses of red water, varying from quite hot to mildly hot and just warm, and a thermometer. With the very young children we had just a glass of very cold water, and a glass of warm water, and they just had to dip their finger in both glasses and tell me which was hot and which was cold, and that was it. With the next batch of slightly older children, I took two glasses of warm and two of cold water and they simply had to tell me which was the hotter of the two and the colder of the two, and I used the thermometer to tell them the same, just drawing their attention to the fact that heat and cold can be measured by a thermometer. I

got a great deal of joy from most of the older ones (ready for Infant). They could compare the three glasses of hot water and cold water, arranging them in the right order, though their language was not perfect – "more hot", "less hot", middle one" – it was quite clear what they meant. I used the thermometer to tell them which was the hottest etc. etc. Children already had some experience, their parent or doctor had used one when they were unwell and quite hot (had a temperature) so we talked a bit about that. They saw the mercury shooting up in hot water and contracting in cold water. After a few days I started talking about it again, they connected thermometer with temperature, like time with clock, they could not use either, but understood the link.

Separating beads out of sand

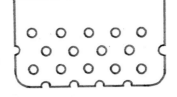 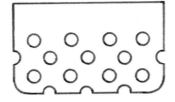 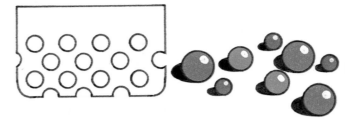

We added three different sizes of beads, smallest red, middle size green and large size blue to the sand. Three sieves with different sized holes were also placed in the sand. I could either ask the children to separate all three sizes of beads, using smallest holed sieve or blue and green beads using the next bigger holed sieve or just blue using the largest sieve. This was science work "separating constituents of a mixture" in a very simple way, and at the same time it was a "matching exercise" selecting the right sieve for the size of the beads, which forms a very important part of nursery teaching. (Sand should not be damp, otherwise it gets stuck in the holes of the sieve). Older children found this activity quite easy, but the younger ones needed a bit of help.

Dissolving substances in water

For some children it was just a pleasant experience of stirring a substance in water with a spoon, while there were others who noticed that not everything dissolves in water. When we started I told them that before you start with a new substance, first dissolve the one you already have, and if they couldn't they would say "but it doesn't go away". After a few times some did realise that not everything disappears in water. The substances provided for children should either be *completely soluble* i.e. salt crystals, white sugar cubes or *insoluble* like rice, sand (washed and dried beforehand) not flour etc., it confuses them.

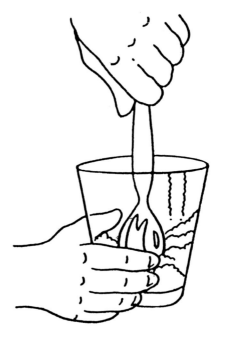

Water play

Displacing water by blowing into the container

This was an immensely enjoyable activity, it added a bit of sparkle to water play. Setting up is very simple but children cannot do it by themselves, it has to be set up by an adult. A is a large transparent plastic sweet jar, B a large round margarine pot (A and B can be any suitable containers). I made a hole in the bottom of B and another hole in the side, and put it upside down in the water trough, A was filled with water and in an inverted position placed on to B while still underwater, otherwise the water flows out. One end of the rubber tubing was introduced into A through B, child blows in through the other end, as he does, the water comes down. Children found this a very enjoyable activity.

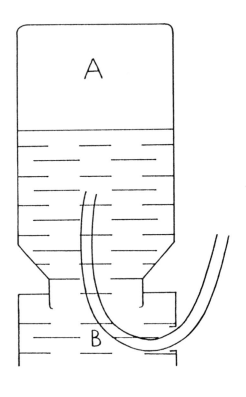

Water play

Making a siphon

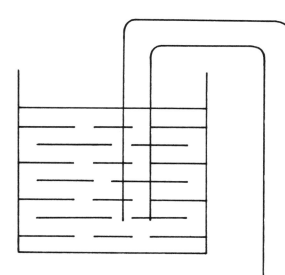

Children cannot get the siphon working, they just have to enjoy what they can do with it. As the siphon emptied the container they filled it up with water, so they had to be pretty quick to keep it going, and that was fun for a lot of them. To start the siphon the tubing can either be filled with water and inverted very quickly in the container or sucked at one end to start the flow of water. Once the water starts flowing it will continue so long as the end of the tube is below the level of the water in the container. It is not very difficult, most people are familiar with the use of a siphon for removing water from fish aquariums or other receptacles which cannot otherwise be emptied conveniently.

Water Play

Floating and sinking

Children used the words "stays down" for sinking and "stays up" for floating. My aim in this experiment was to show them that some things float while others sink. I had a large container full of things that would float or sink, and two trays, one for articles that would sink, the other one for articles that would float. We had only one or two children working at a time, they would pick the object, see if it floated or sank, and then put it in the appropriate tray. This was done very successfully, even by the younger children, but it does need some supervision otherwise one is likely to get the odd unruly child splashing things in the water. Apart from a science experience, this is a usual "sorting" activity, which is part of nursery teaching.

Symmetry

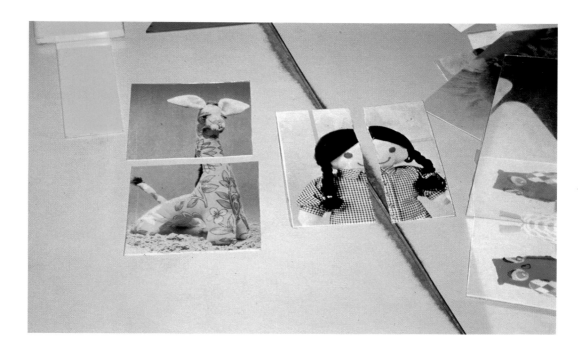

I cut up into two parts symmetrical and asymmetrical pictures (mounted on cardboard) as shown in picture 1. Children tried putting them together to complete the picture. After a little while I showed them another way of completing the picture using a mirror, they also tried, for the symmetrical ones they said "I can make it" otherwise "can't make it", I told them that if they can make it, it's called symmetrical, and left it at that, this is enough for nursery children.

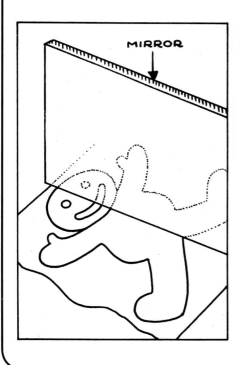

Making a bulb light

The apparatus was arranged as shown in the diagram, when the two ends of the battery were touched with crocodile clips the bulb lit up, providing immense pleasure to the child. One girl asked me what made the bulb light, was there fire in the battery? I couldn't give her the correct answer (she couldn't possibly understand that) so I just smiled. There were some who used more than one battery. One little girl used six batteries, like the rest she did not understand the positive and negative of batteries, but managed the right way round by trial and error, she looked the other way, and I changed the end batteries the other way round, unable to light the bulb, she started from scratch again, with one battery, two, three and so on everytime seeing if the bulb lit.

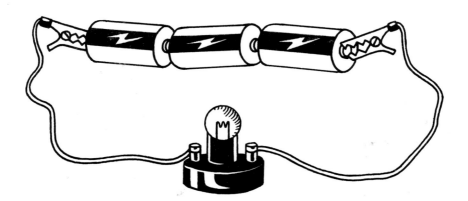

Switching on the lights in a doll's house

We set up a simple circuit like before, but instead of the bulb being left as in the previous case, we placed a little doll's house over it, children found it more fun to light up a doll's house rather than a mere bulb. We compared it to lights at home and in the classroom. They started with one battery and then as many as they could manage. The more the batteries, the brighter the light shone through the house window. Even though I did not spell out everything, it was beginning to make sense to a lot of the children, especially the older ones, although they did not know negative and positive of the battery, if the light was not switched on, they would try changing the batteries around.

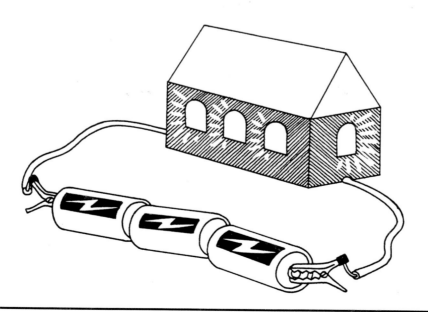

Conductors and insulators

I did not mention the above two words, a circuit was set up as shown in the diagram. At the point B where the two crocodile clips touch, we introduced all sorts of things – metal, non-metal etc. Children collected things from all over the classroom, this was a very exciting experiment. Two children worked on this, one dealt with the batteries while the other tested the object. If the bulb lit it was "O.K. thing" (conductors) otherwise "not O.K. thing" (insulators). At least they realised that there are O.K. and not O.K. materials.

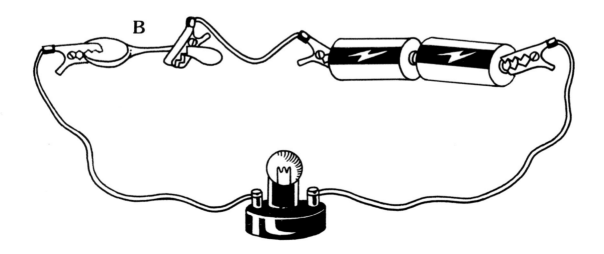

Magnets

Finding objects that are attracted by a magnet

We had three trays, one with a mixture of small metal and non-metal objects, the other two left empty, one for the things that would be attracted by the magnet and the other for the ones not attracted by it. Children took one object at a time, put it on the table and touched it with the magnet, then depending on whether it was attracted by the magnet or not, put it in the appropriate tray. The older children seemed to understand somewhat the sort of things that would be attracted to the magnet, invariably they would pick up metallic stuff, try it with the magnet just to confirm and then put it in the right tray. The younger ones did try each one, without any idea of how it would work. Apart from getting them to find out about the properties of magnets, it also is a usual nursery activity – sorting categorizing.

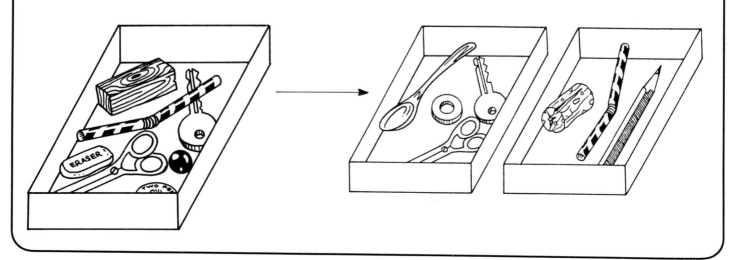

Magnets

Separating constituents of a mixture using a magnet

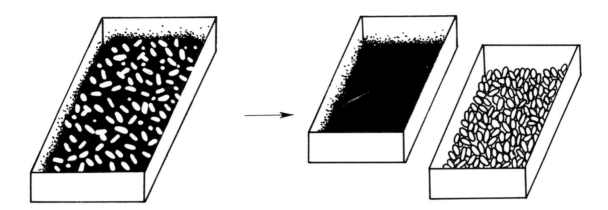

We put the mixture of iron filings and rice in a tray and as the children moved the magnets in the mixture, the iron filings clung on to them, which were scraped off into another tray, this was repeated until we had almost separated the mixture. It was a very popular activity. I also used a very strong round magnet, the iron filings clung on to it giving it an appearance of a tiny hedgehog, some children were literally scared of touching it, after a little while they got over it.

Magnets and iron filings

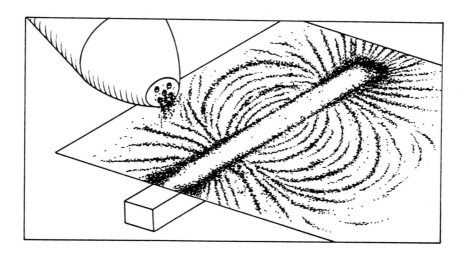

We put the magnet underneath the paper, it was thin and white , and sprinkled iron filings from a pepper pot on to the paper, they were immediately arranged in a lovely pattern. This depends on the strength of the magnetic field and the shape of the magnet. The filings get arranged along the "lines of magnetic force". Quite a few children got "hooked" on this activity, they would put the filings back in the pot and start it all over again, sometimes with a different shaped magnet. It was a lively activity.

Making a Magnet

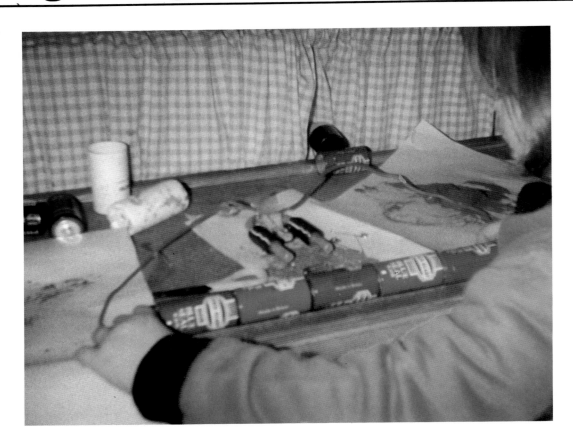

After the children became quite familiar with making a simple circuit work, and magnets, I introduced electro-magnet. When the circuit is complete the horseshoe shaped "object" becomes a magnet. I did teach them the word electro-magnet. When the magnet was held in the air, and then the circuit broken all the things previously stuck to it fell off, and that was fun, then they would repeat it again and again. If iron filings are used and the circuit is completed and broken off quickly, the iron filings cling and then drop off, producing a "jumpy effect". Children enjoyed this activity very much.

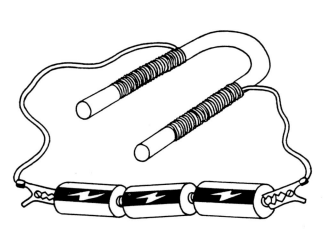

Animals

I would only keep small animals (invertebrates) in the class, because children can see the life cycle and then they can be set free, I don't like the idea of children seeing "caged animals" as something normal, cruelty to animals should be discouraged right from the start. I had quite a few magnifying jars in my classroom, children liked to see tiny things i.e. butterfly eggs, flies, spiders, magnified, and since they cannot focus properly with a magnifying glass, these jars are a good idea to have, animals must not be left in the jars for more than a few seconds otherwise they could die of suffocation.

Animals

Borrowing animals from other places like science centres, pet shops or laboratories is a very good idea, even parents or friends sometimes have unusual pets. Some animals carry a risk of infection, this should be checked beforehand. Our nursery nurse managed to borrow a snake from a local pet shop, children played with it all day and then we returned it. They found it very exciting, and I got bombarded with all sorts of questions, like what does he eat, does he do 'wee wee' (excrete). They also asked how does he move, he does not have any legs, and whether it was a boy or girl.

We managed to get a rabbit from a science institution for the day, and that caused quite a sensation. Children spent a lot of time in front of the cage. For inner city children this is an unusual experience. We also had just for the day a Guinea pig, gerbil, various kinds of birds including a duck.

Making a home for worms

We borrowed a Wormery from a junior school and set up a table with sand, ordinary soil dug up from where we were going to hunt for earth worms, and some chalk plus a little water to make the layers of soil, sand and chalk damp, moist, but not too wet. Children filled up the wormery with layers of these materials and then we went into the garden and dug up some earthworms. They thoroughly enjoyed the task. Back in the classroom we put the earthworms in the wormery and a few dead leaves, then covered the wormery with black paper. After 2 weeks we took the black paper off the wormery, there were tunnels in the soil and hardly any in the sand and chalk. Some children asked me why didn't they make tunnels in the sand, I said because the worms prefer soil to anything else.

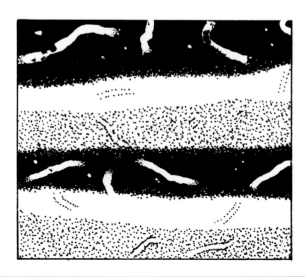

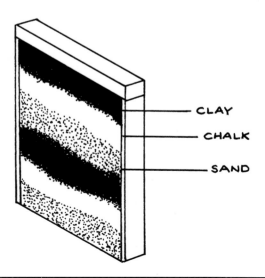

CLAY

CHALK

SAND

Stick insects

A lot of children took to stick insects very readily, there were some who only watched from a distance, however I did not force anyone because in the long run it doesn't help. We counted the insect's legs, looked at their antennae, eyes, etc, and there were quite a few questions, like "do they talk" etc. To add to our interest some new ones

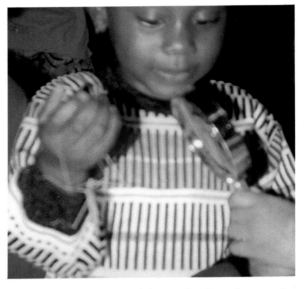

hatched out, one moulted and two died. Children helped me in cleaning (I did not involve them directly), giving fresh leaves and making sure they were warm and comfortable. If one insect did not look too healthy or was too still, they reported the matter to me with great concern. Involvement with animals is very important, so that they become aware right from the start that animals have needs too, they eat, drink and excrete just like humans.

Spiders

This proved to be far more exciting than I first thought, we set up an empty fish tank with a few twigs, peat at the bottom and a little container with a few drops of water. Children were not involved with catching the spiders, I did that job with a parent. These were garden spiders, one rather large and five small ones. Spiders lived on crickets which I bought from a local pet shop, and the crickets lived on raw and cooked potatoes. Some adults thought I was being cruel, but children take such things much better. Overnight, to our surprise, one of the spiders spun a web, later on we had more. One spider (the fat one) laid lots of eggs in a white cocoon and died. The following Spring lots of little spiders hatched out of the eggs. Crickets did make a little noise sometimes, it formed a nice contrast to the artificial, synthetic play stuff in the classroom.

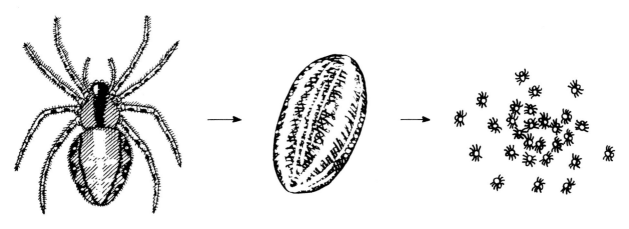

Hatching chicken eggs

This caused a lot of excitement in the nursery, children were simply fascinated by the way chickens start pecking on the shell when they are about to come out, and then the shell gradually splits open and out comes a slightly wet chicken, which slowly fluffs up to look like a yellow ball of cotton wool, even better than that. The next thing they did after being removed from the incubator was to make a "little mess". One little boy asked me "Are they allowed to wee-wee? (excrete)". Gradually they started eating, a girl from a very religious background said "But they didn't bless their food". Hatching eggs needs considerable planning because one wouldn't like the chickens to hatch at the weekend, although they don't always hatch at the right time, one should plan it so that they are due on any day from Monday to Friday. The next thing was, where would they go after they hatch? This has to be sorted out first. We gave ours to another nursery and someone who wanted to rear chickens for eggs.

Hatching chicken eggs

Sometimes people just take them because they look nice and the next thing you know is that "they got sick and died". This has to be worked out very carefully, preferably given to a farm. Things can go wrong during 21 days of incubation, therefore it would be advisable to get eggs from a farm which are very near hatching, and possibly return the chicks to them after hatching, it could save a lot of headache. Finally, one question which some little one asked me which I did not answer – "why doesn't a chicken come out of my egg that I have for breakfast." Saying that it had to be kept warm for sometime was not a complete answer, fertile egg part is very difficult to explain, so I thought it was best to leave it and let them find out when they are a bit older.

Butterflies

We ordered butterfly eggs from a company that supplies "living materials" to institutions. Butterfly eggs are like little dots, and arrived through the post in a little petri dish on a cabbage leaf. Children had to look at them through the magnifying glass. Next day they had all hatched out, still barely visible to the naked eye. After three to four days they became tiny green caterpillars which were

making holes in the cabbage leaves. The caterpillars grew bigger and bigger, ate a lot of cabbage and produced a lot of droppings – quite smelly! After some time the caterpillars changed into pupae, which unlike caterpillars did not eat or move, and were very still, and out of these came the butterflies, which we set free in the park, children found

Butterflies

the whole life cycle exciting. I had a very big chart of the life cycle of butterfly, it helped to explain to children at what stage "they were" and what was going to happen next, it was amazing that the children could follow it so easily.

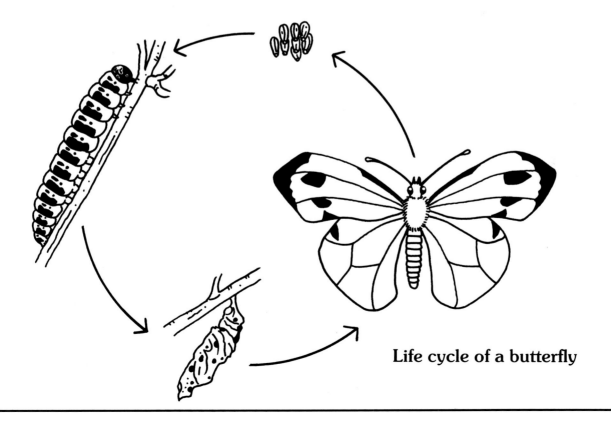

Life cycle of a butterfly

Moths

The life cycle of a moth is pretty much the same as the butterfly. We bought eggs, black in colour, from a butterfly farm. The caterpillars were beautiful, large, green with black dots, and the children played about with them. We fed them with Willow leaves. After some time caterpillars went into a resting stage pupae, these were quite big, oval and dark brown in colour, this phase lasted quite long, and finally the bright coloured moths appeared.

Growing mushrooms

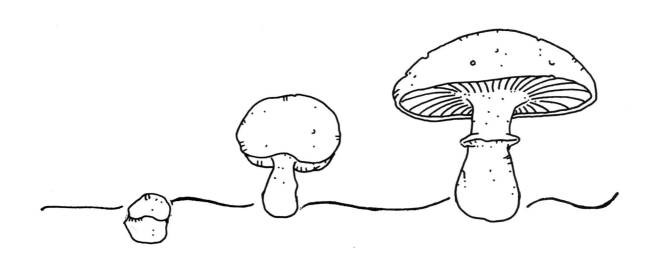

The best time to grow mushrooms is straight after the summer holidays, because we still get fairly warm days off and on. They can be grown straight from the spores sold in a packet or some nurseries do the "ready mix", spores with the right sort of soil and some manure-like substance, with all necessary instructions using specific temperatures at different stages etc. Children found this very exciting. In the end we made omelette with the mushrooms that we had grown.

Growing seeds in a pumpkin

This experiment should be in Spring or Summer, and the pumpkin used should be very fresh. The seeds we used, cress and bean, were soaked for 24 hours and then transferred to the sprouter and left there for a couple of days, about a dozen holes were made in the pumpkin. The seeds were lifted very carefully with the root end (base) pointing downward and placed into the holes in the pumpkin. Within a short time the roots started growing in the pumpkin. This growth did not last very long, but provided a nice experience for the children. Seedlings were given drops of water with a pipette occasionally to prevent drying, a little plasticine was used at the point where the root goes down into the pumpkin to prevent air going inside it, otherwise the pumpkin rots very quickly.

Growing seeds in a marrow

Seeds grow very easily in a marrow, I removed a rectangular piece from a marrow ¼" × 2" × 1" and carefully placed the already germinated cress seeds on the white fleshy part and then added a few drops of water. Within a couple of days the cress started to grow as shown in the picture below. I gave them a few drops of water about twice a day. Children were fascinated by this experiment.

Growing tomatoes in the classroom

We grew tomatoes in an old discarded "sand trough" which we placed near the window for maximum sunshine. Children took turns to water the plants to which special tomato food was added. The plants grew fast, and we had yellow flowers that dropped off and the inner part of the flower turned into tiny green tomatoes. There is a slight difficulty in growing tomatoes inside the classroom because the flowers are not visited by many insects, and so I had to pollinate them myself, by squeezing the flower gently so that the outer part (stamen)

touched the inner part (carpel). Children behaved in a very responsible way, watering the plants regularly, nobody picked any flowers or tomatoes. They kept reporting how many more we had, size and colour. Children really got involved in this activity, this is especially good for those living in flats or inner city, who never see much of plant life.

Plants drink water

White daffodils were put in water to which food colouring had been added, flowers in red coloured water had reddish tint, yellow a little yellow, and blue somewhat blue. This was a little experiment to show that plants take up water. I did explain to the children that like we give animals (pets) food we give water to the plants otherwise they die, hoping that this would make them think about watering any indoor plants that they may have at home.

Matching game with plants

This is best done in Spring. I collected all sorts of wild plants, flowers and leaves from trees, which were easy to recognise. I then prepared cards with flower and leaf specimens by sticking them on the card and then covering them with thin plastic covering. The same afternoon we took the children to the area where I had originally collected the specimens, and asked them to match the cards with the flowers and leaves, which they did very easily. An occasional activity like this would help the children to get to know the vegetation of their environment which I feel is very important.

Showing root, stem and leaves

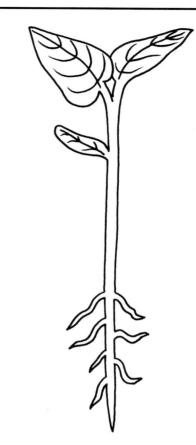

We grew bean seeds in jam jars. This little experiment is good for showing that the roots go down while the shoot (stem and leaves) grow upward, almost always. We filled the jam jars with paper towel and water, and very carefully placed the bean seeds between the glass and paper towel, and soon had little plants. I asked a boy why the roots don't grow upwards, out came a very stern spontaneous reply "because they can't". I couldn't have answered this any better.

A few days after this experiment I repotted plants with children explaining to them why the plants needed bigger containers by now they had become familiar with the words root, stem and leaves and seem to understand my explanation. There are always plants in the school that need repotting.

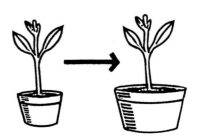

Plants grow towards light

I painted a plastic tray half bright yellow and planted wheat in it with children's help. We placed the tray near the window. The little seedlings as they grew, were bent towards the window, I drew children's attention to this, and moved the tray the other way around, after a fortnight or more, the plants became bent the other way round, and then we talked about why this happened. A little girl said because they like to look out of the window, I said I think they like the sunlight and left it at that.

Growing potatoes

We grew potatoes in an old fish tank, covered it up with black paper. The potatoes used had already started sprouting, they had been left in a dark damp place for some time. We soon had a sort of creeper, which had to be supported by big sticks, and later fixed to the wall by a string. After about 12 weeks the plants started getting brown (withering). At that point we pulled the plants out of the container, they had small pink potatoes, which we boiled and had them with salt and pepper, they tasted delicious. It was a good experience for children since they had not seen potatoes growing anywhere before.

Growing beans

 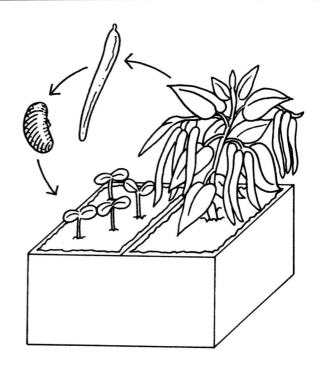

We grew lots of seeds in an old discarded water trough, only half of the trough was used at first. The plants grew quite quickly, it was late Spring/Summer. Children observed the appearance of flowers which dropped (petals) and then small beans grew bigger and bigger. We left a few on the plants for seeds, and eventually we used these seeds on the other half of the trough. Children planted them, and we got new plants in a short time. In this way they got to see the whole life cycle.

A child planting seeds taken from the mother plant

Keeping Ladybirds

In the spring, April/May, with the help of some children, I collected lots of ladybirds and put them in a very large plastic jar. The jar had been prepared beforehand, with a plant being placed in the jar (growing in a container). Lots of very tiny holes were made in the jar because both the ladybirds and the plants need air. Placing leaves would have been easier, but replacing them would have been very difficult because each leaf would have to be examined very carefully so that neither the ladybirds or their eggs were lost with the leaves. The plant was watered twice a week, I also left a tiny plate with a few drops of water, but never saw ladybirds drinking it and I supplied a lot of aphids (green fly). The jar must not be left in bright sunshine because that makes the ladybirds very restless and they go round and round looking for shade.

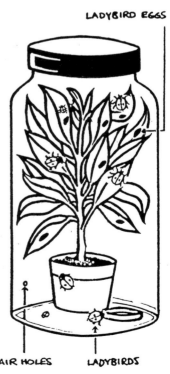

LADYBIRD EGGS

AIR HOLES   LADYBIRDS

Ladybirds

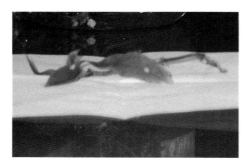

Within a day or two the ladybirds started laying eggs in clusters on the leaves and also on the side of the jar. They were bright yellow and shaped like skittles. After a few days very tiny black larvae came out of these eggs. I transferred these to another jar and fed them with ground beef, but one has to make sure that there is no fat in it, otherwise the larvae legs get stuck in the fat and they cannot move.

I found that the ladybirds we caught would not eat ground beef, but the larvae which were given this food from the start accepted it quite readily. This beef must be changed at least twice a day, because the meat can rot very quickly, which produces odours, and one wouldn't want the larvae to go off their food. There must be ample supply of food otherwise the bigger larvae start living on the weaker and smaller ones, and the number would diminish rapidly.

After some days the larvae passed into pupae stage, in which they did not eat or walk about. They appeared as a grey/blackish oval mess with very faint stripes and appear to be lifeless, but when I touched one of them with a sharp pointed pencil, it moved.

After about two weeks the skin of the pupae split and pale looking ladybirds emerged. The children and I took them out to the park and set them free. The complete life cycle is shown in the diagram below.

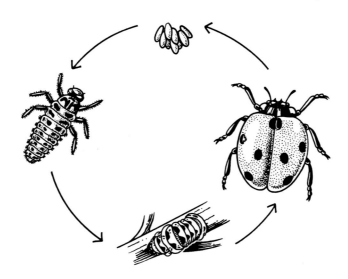